PEER GYNT

SUITES NOS. 1 AND 2
in Full Score

EDVARD GRIEG

DOVER PUBLICATIONS, INC.
Mineola, New York

Bibliographical Note

This Dover edition, first published in 1997, is an unabridged republication of an early authoritative score, n.d. The Dover edition adds lists of contents and instrumentation and English translations of the original German footnotes.

International Standard Book Number: 0-486-29582-6

Manufactured in the United States of America
Dover Publications, Inc., 31 East 2nd Street, Mineola, N.Y. 11501

In 1874, Henrik Ibsen invited Edvard Grieg to compose incidental music for a staged version of his great Norwegian verse drama *Peer Gynt*. That work was first performed in Christiania (now Oslo) on 24 February 1876. Grieg rescored his incidental music for an 1886 production, then selected eight of the twenty-two pieces for the two orchestral suites of 1888 and 1891.

CONTENTS

INSTRUMENTATION

Piccolo [Flauto piccolo, Fl. pic.]

2 Flutes [Flauti gr(andi), Fl.]
  Flute 2 doubles Piccolo 2

2 Oboes [Oboi, Ob.]

2 Clarinets in A, B♭ ("B") [Clarinetti, Cl.]

2 Bassoons [Fagotti, Fag.]

4 Horns in E, F [Corni, Cor.]

2 Trumpets in E, F [Trombe, Tbe.]

3 Trombones [2 Tromboni Tenori (Trbn. T.)
  (later, Alto & Tenore); Trombone Basso (Trbn. B.)]

Tuba [Tuba, Tb.]

Timpani [Timpani, Timp.; Pk. (Pauken)]

Percussion:
  Triangle [Triangolo, Tria.]
  Cymbals [Piatti, Pia.]
  Tambourine [Tamburino, Tam.]
  Small Drum [Tamburo piccolo, Ta. pic.]
  Bass Drum & Cymbals [Gran Cassa e Piatti, Pia.]

Harp [Arpa]

Violins I, II [Violini, Vl.]

Violas [Viole, Vle.]

Cellos [Violoncelli, Vc.]

Basses [Bassi, Cb.]

PEER GYNT SUITE NO. 1

1. Morning Mood

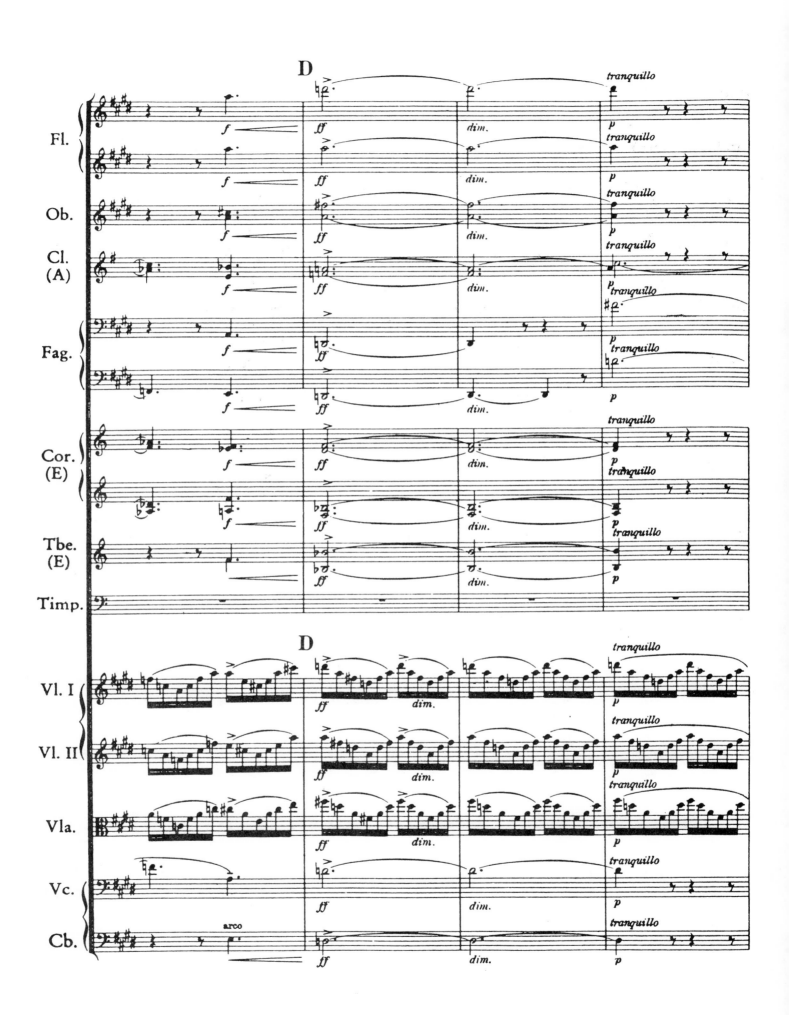

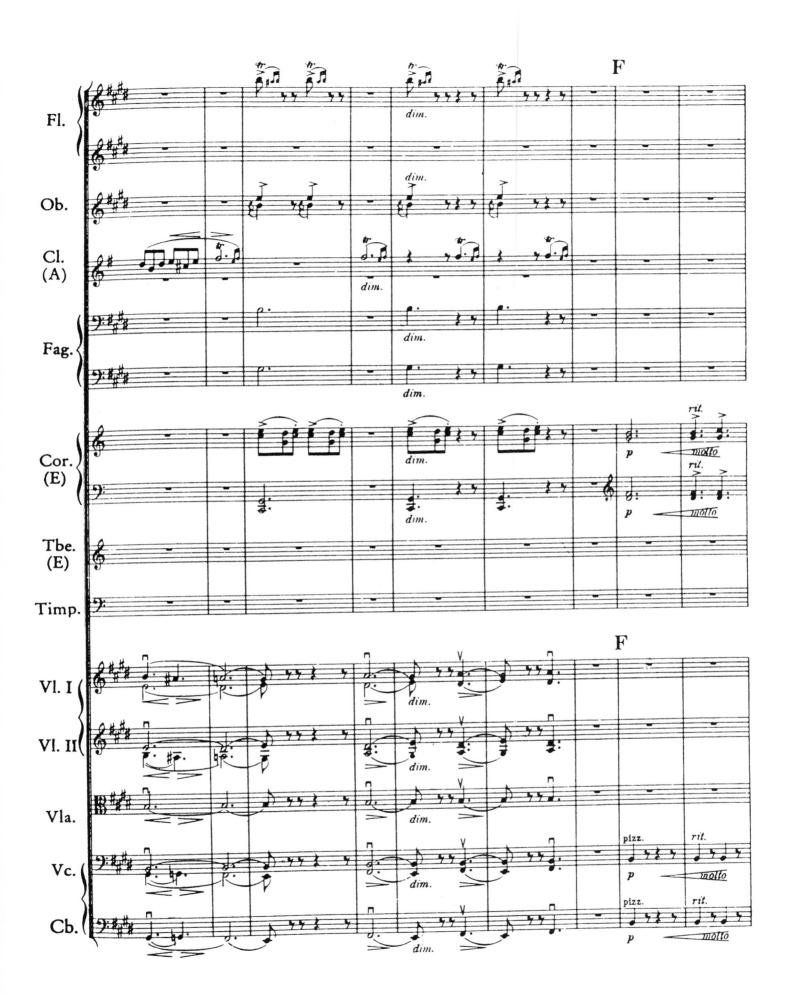

2. Aase's Death

3. Anitra's Dance

[Can also be performed by 9 soloists (2 Vl. I, 2 Vl. II, 2 Vla., 2 Vc. and 1 Cb.)]
*[The trills are to be performed without Nachschlag (grace notes that follow a trill)]

4. In the Hall of the Mountain King

[NB. + = stopped tone]

PEER GYNT SUITE NO. 2

1. The Abduction of the Bride
(Ingrid's Lament)

[NB. + = stopped tone]

2. Arabian Dance

*[The two-part pizz. must here be performed not as an arpeggio but with two fingers of the right hand.]

* [The two-part pizz. must here be performed not as an arpeggio but with two fingers of the right hand.]

Arabian Dance

3. Peer Gynt's Journey Home

Peer Gynt's Journey Home

4. Solveig's Song

*[very delicately, the 16th notes not too short]

END OF EDITION